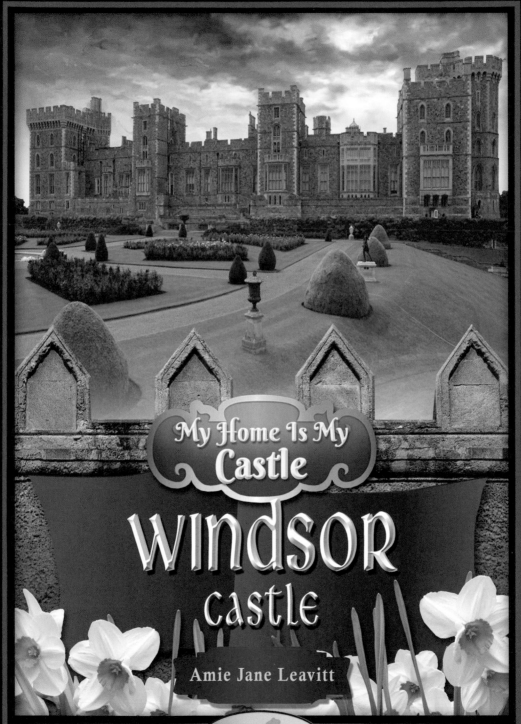

My Home Is My
Castle

windsor
castle

Amie Jane Leavitt

PURPLE TOAD
PUBLISHING

My Home Is My Castle

BALMORAL CASTLE by Amie Jane Leavitt
GLAMIS CASTLE by Tammy Gagne
HEARST CASTLE by Ann Tatlock
VERSAILLES by Amie Jane Leavitt
WINDSOR CASTLE by Amie Jane Leavitt

PUBLISHER'S NOTE
The data in this book has been researched in depth, and to the best of our knowledge is factual. Although every measure is taken to give an accurate account, Purple Toad Publishing makes no warranty of the accuracy of the information and is not liable for damages caused by inaccuracies.

ABOUT THE AUTHOR
Amie Jane Leavitt is an accomplished author, researcher, and photographer. She graduated from Brigham Young University as an education major and has since taught all subjects and grade levels in both private and public schools. She is an adventurer who loves to travel the globe in search of interesting story ideas and beautiful places to capture in photos. She has written more than fifty books for kids, has contributed to online and print media, and has worked as a consultant, writer, and editor for numerous educational publishing and assessment companies. Leavitt is fascinated by world history, especially British history, and has toured Great Britain. For that reason, she particularly enjoyed researching and writing this book about Windsor Castle. Check out a listing of Leavitt's current projects and published works at www.amiejaneleavitt.com.

Printing   1   2   3   4   5   6   7   8   9

Publisher's Cataloging-in-Publication data
Leavitt, Amie Jane.
  Windsor castle / Amie Jane Leavitt.
    p. cm.
Includes bibliographic references and index.
ISBN 9781624691423
1. Windsor Castle—History—Juvenile literature. 2. Castles—Great Britain—Juvenile literature. I. Series: My home is my castle.
DA690 2015
914.2

2014946228

eBook ISBN: 9781624691430

contents

Introduction
FIRE!

The morning of Friday, November 20, 1992, started out just like any other at Windsor Castle. The staff went about their duties preparing for the Queen's arrival that evening. It was the 45th anniversary of her marriage to Prince Philip, and they were coming to her weekend retreat to celebrate. The only member of the royal family at Windsor that morning was Prince Andrew, Queen Elizabeth and Prince Philip's son, who had spent the previous night there.

At 11:33 A.M., a staff member ran down the royal corridor of the castle's northeast wing. "Fire!" he shouted. A picture had been propped against the wall in Queen Victoria's Chapel, pressing a curtain against a 1,000-watt spotlight. The fabric ignited, and the fire quickly spread. The chapel and surrounding rooms filled with smoke and flames. The castle's 20-man firefighting team rushed to the scene. On their way, they alerted the Royal Berkshire Fire and Rescue Service. Fire trucks were dispatched.[1]

Prince Andrew, who was in the opposite end of the castle, didn't hear the commotion and screams of "fire," but he did hear the fire alarm. He dashed out of the castle and saw smoke billowing into the sky. He rushed toward the northeast wing and joined a team of castle staff, town residents, and military men who were quickly trying to remove as many precious items as possible from the castle before they were destroyed.

It was a heartbreaking scene for the castle staff, royal family members, and townspeople to watch their beloved Windsor Castle being swallowed up by flames. Luckily, the damage to the castle during the 1992 fire was minimal.

Every room of the castle was filled with masterpieces and national heirlooms. If they were destroyed by fire, they could never be replaced. "There was little time to think of anything else," Prince Andrew later told a news crew.[2]

The rescuers formed a human chain, passing state furniture, boxes of jewelry, paintings, and books from person to person, out the castle windows and down to the courtyard below. The fire spread quickly and the fire crews—35 fire trucks and 225 men—worked tirelessly to extinguish the blaze. Putting out the fire proved to be very difficult. The 900-year-old castle was riddled with secret passageways and dusty nooks and crannies that helped the fire travel. In these behind-the-walls-and-ceilings spaces, the flames ate hungrily through the old timbers and wooden framework of the structure. Within an hour, the fire had spread to St. George's Hall and the largest of the State Apartments.

When St. George's Hall was renovated after the 1992 fire, the shields of the Knights of the Garter (seen here hanging on the walls) were recreated. The originals were destroyed in the fire.

The fire was devastating to certain areas of the castle. Yet, it was all eventually completely restored.

By 1:30 P.M., the fire crews had constructed firebreaks at the southern wall of the Green Drawing Room and at the northwest corner of Chester Tower. These breaks would help stop the fire from spreading to other parts of the castle.

Night fell around 4:15 that evening. The flames from the castle shot more than 50 feet into the night sky. People for miles around could watch the blaze directly, and people around the world watched the castle burn throughout the night on television.

It took more than nine hours to subdue the fire and another three hours to completely extinguish it. The fire crews used over a million gallons of water fighting the fire, much of which came from the nearby River Thames. Nearly 10,000 square feet (more than 9,000 square meters), or about one-fifth of the castle, had been either damaged or destroyed. That included more than 100 rooms—nine of which were principal rooms in the structure.

By the next morning, the damage was more visible. The Queen came to see it firsthand and was distraught by what she saw. So were the townspeople.

"I'm absolutely devastated," one woman told a news reporter. "I love the royal family. I love Windsor. I live here [in the town of Windsor] because I love Windsor. It is my home, so this [castle] is my home, too."[3]

*DISCLAIMER: Purple Toad Publishing does not condone entering a burning building for any reason. In the event of a fire, call 911 from a safe place and wait for fire department officials to arrive.

CHAPTER 1

a fortress on a hill

Christmas Day in 1066 was especially delightful for William, the Duke of Normandy. He was crowned the king of England that day, the first English king to hail from his country. His coronation in Westminster Abbey had not been guaranteed. Years earlier, in 1051, King Edward of England had promised to bestow the throne on William, yet when Edward died in early 1066, another man, Harold, Earl of Wessex, claimed the throne for himself. On September 28, 1066, William sailed across the English Channel and invaded England in order to claim his rightful title. On October 14, a battle ensued between the two men's armies, and the Norman duke was victorious.

William the Conqueror's victory at the Battle of Hastings secured his place in history as the first Norman king of England.

William the Conqueror

When he was crowned king of England, he was known as William the Conqueror.[1]

A few years later, in 1070, William was out hunting in the royal forest near the River Thames. As he rode up to the top of a high cliff, he decided it would be the perfect spot to build a castle. From this vantage point, his soldiers could adequately protect him and his court. After all, on a clear day, they could see for miles in every direction. The castle would be part of a ring of nine forts that surrounded London, blocking invaders who tried to approach the capital city from the west. The nearby Thames could also be used to transport troops from the castle to London very quickly.

Construction on the castle—which would be known as Windsor Castle—began immediately. It took 16 years for William's men to complete this phase of the project.[2]

The castle's construction would continue for hundreds of years, however. Windsor Castle is still, to this day, a work in progress. It covers an enormous piece of land—nearly 13 acres. Most castles built during the time period of William the Conqueror covered only 4 or 5 acres. In this space, there is the castle and all its buildings, and also an impressive number of gardens. In modern times, the 35-acre Savill Garden is part of the Windsor Great Park directly next to the castle grounds, yet it is considered part of the Windsor Castle experience.

The castle that William built was constructed in the motte-and-bailey style. A motte is a mound of soil that is created when a ditch, or moat, is dug. At the top of the motte, the workers built a keep, or the castle's square main tower. From this tower, they could "keep" watch on the surrounding area. The bailey was a large fenced courtyard that surrounded the motte, barracks, and other buildings and was designed to protect the keep.

William the Conqueror never really *lived* at Windsor. It was considered more of a fortress than a home during his time. Henry I, William's youngest son, did spend some of his holidays there (Christmas and Easter), and he eventually kept his court at the castle for many months at a time. In January 1121, Henry married Adeliza of Louvain at Windsor—they were the first couple to wed at the castle. Henry continued to visit the castle many more times during his reign. His last visit was in Christmas 1133, about two years before his death.[3]

The majority of the castle that was built by William the Conqueror's men was constructed out of timber from the nearby forest. When compared to sturdier building materials, wood really isn't the best choice. First, it can burn easily, and fires were a major concern in medieval times. Second, invaders could break through it with nothing more than common picks and axes. The monarchs who served after William's reign knew they had to improve the castle's fortifications.

During the 1170s, King Henry II put his crews to work replacing the outer fences and the walls of the keep, using stone instead of wood.[4] He also decided to change the shape of the keep. Square was a poor idea for a tower, because people could sneak around the corners and hide. Making the tower round would not only eliminate the corners, but it would also distribute the weight of the tower more evenly. This was a crucial advantage, because the new tower, built of stone, would be a lot heavier than the old wooden tower. In addition, according to local folklore, the legendary King Arthur had placed his famous

King Henry II

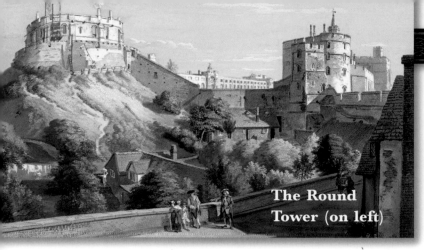

The Round Tower (on left)

round table on this spot to discuss matters of the kingdom with his knights.[5] It seemed appropriate that a round tower be built here, in honor of England's most beloved king.

Henry II was the first monarch to turn the castle into a palace fit for a royal family. He had two sets of royal apartments constructed: one was the State Apartments, or official residences; the other was the private apartments.[6] Today, the ancient Round Tower stores the Royal Archives and the Royal Photograph Collection.

King John, who was crowned in 1199, spent a lot of his time at Windsor Castle—months and months at a stretch. Yet, he wasn't spending his time relaxing. Trouble was brewing in England, and King John was right in the middle of it. In recent battles, John had lost a large amount of England's land in Normandy. He wanted it back. In order to do that, he needed money, and lots of it. The easiest and best way to get money at that time was to tax the people. If he wanted the money quickly, which he did, he had to be ruthless about his taxation and collection practices.

No one was happy about the heavy taxes or John's methods of attaining them. His barons, who were especially unhappy, tried talking to the king to bring him to his senses, but in the end, negotiations proved unsuccessful. Civil war looked like the only option. At one point in early 1215, rebels seized London, and John was forced to hole up in Windsor. Finally, on June 15, John agreed to meet with the barons in a field called Runnymede, an area a few miles south of the castle. There, John agreed to sign a treaty with the barons. Called the Magna Carta, this document was the first in known history that limited the rights of a monarch. Essentially, it stated that a government has laws, and even the king has to obey them. This revolutionary document, signed not too far from Windsor Castle, was so significant in its ideas that it was eventually used as a guide for American patriots seeking independence from Britain.[7]

MEDIEVAL ARMOR

Jousting armor of Henry III

During medieval times, soldiers wore suits of armor. These helped protect their bodies during hand-to-hand combat. Even the horses generally wore some kind of armor—such as a face-, neck-, and breastplate. Some knights also covered their horse's haunches with metal. Generally, the underside and the legs of the horse were not covered. A man in battle who lost his horse was essentially a dead man, so protecting his horse was of the utmost importance.

The royal collection at Windsor Castle features many suits of armor. One full-body suit dates to 1563 and is made of heavy plates of steel. It has a helmet with a face shield that can open and close. Another suit from the same period is made a little differently. The armor on the legs reaches only to the knees, and the arms have chainmail instead of armor plates. Other suits in the collection include small suits that would have been worn by teenage squires and child pages. The collection also has large suits that would have fit the more robust men in England, like King Henry VIII. The knights would have also carried shields to protect themselves from the enemy's swords, clubs, and maces.

These suits of armor might have helped protect knights, but they must have been hard to move in. In 2011, BBC News reported on a team of scientists who studied the human body's movement while wearing a suit of armor. People were tested by walking on treadmills while wearing suits of armor. The scientists found that it takes twice as much energy for the average person to either walk or run while wearing a suit of armor.

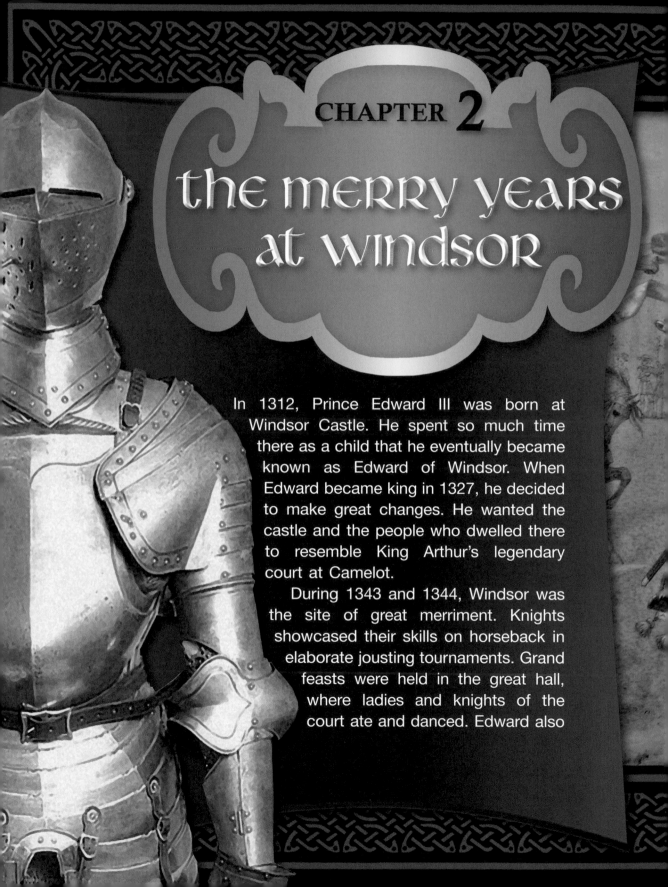

CHAPTER 2

the merry years at windsor

In 1312, Prince Edward III was born at Windsor Castle. He spent so much time there as a child that he eventually became known as Edward of Windsor. When Edward became king in 1327, he decided to make great changes. He wanted the castle and the people who dwelled there to resemble King Arthur's legendary court at Camelot.

During 1343 and 1344, Windsor was the site of great merriment. Knights showcased their skills on horseback in elaborate jousting tournaments. Grand feasts were held in the great hall, where ladies and knights of the court ate and danced. Edward also

Knights thrill the crowd during a joust.

held special meetings with his knights at a large round table, just as King Arthur is said to have done.[1]

In 1348, Edward decided to start a new order of knights called the Order of the Garter. This order is still around today and is considered the oldest order of British chivalry. An order is an organization of brotherhood or companionship similar to a fraternity. Only 26 knights could be members of the order, and they were chosen based on certain criteria such as courtesy, generosity, bravery, and victory in battle. The first members of the Order of the Garter met at Windsor Castle in 1349 for the feast of St. George. In the same year, Edward III also founded two new colleges, which were essentially communities of priests. One was the college of St. Stephen at Westminster Palace, and the other was the college of St. George at Windsor. The college at Windsor worked directly with the knights of the Garter.[2]

In the 1360s, Edward III started construction on St. George's Hall inside Windsor Castle. (This is the same hall that was damaged some 600 years later by the fire in 1992.) At 182 feet (55.5 meters) long and 30 feet (9 meters) wide, the massive hall was intended for official functions of the Garter Knights. It is about half the length of a football field—although it's doubtful that anyone has ever dared to toss a football in this grand space. On the walls are life-size portraits of the English monarchs from James I (who ruled 1603–1625) to George IV (1830–1837). The hall is also adorned with the coats of armor of the knights of the Garter.[3] The long table used for royal dinners can comfortably seat 160 guests.

Edward set up the spiritual home of the Garter in a chapel on the grounds of Windsor, which he renamed St. George's Chapel. St. George, the patron saint of England, had been well known and revered in the country since around the year 900.[4]

Fast-forward more than one hundred years to the reign of Edward IV. In 1475, he began construction on a new St. George's Chapel, a building that wouldn't be finished for fifty years.[5] This magnificent chapel is still used by the Queen and the Order of the Garter when they meet at Windsor Castle. With its strong vertical lines, St. George's Chapel is considered the finest example in all of England of the Perpendicular style of Gothic architecture.

Today, St. George's Chapel holds worship services every Sunday in addition to special events, exhibitions, and musical performances.

Gothic architecture features height and light. When standing inside the chapel, the fan vault ceilings feel miles away. The interior is bathed in golden light that filters through the chapel's vast stained-glass windows. The chapel is adorned with the badges, banners, helmets, crests, and swords of the knights of the Garter. Another special feature is the roof adorned with stone creatures. Known as the king's beasts, these 76 animals include a bull for bravery, a griffin for vigilance, a unicorn for strength, and a swan for grace and perfection.[6] St. George's Chapel is also the final resting place of members of English royalty, including King Henry VIII and his third wife, Jane Seymour; Charles I; King Edward IV; King George VI; Princess Margaret; and Queen Elizabeth, the Queen Mother, who died in 2002.[7]

One of England's most famous, or infamous, monarchs was King Henry VIII. He acquired his dubious reputation because of his obsession with wanting a male heir to the throne; he was willing to divorce, and behead,

wives who did not produce one for him. During the early years of his reign, Henry spent a great amount of time at Windsor Castle. He loved recreation and entertainment of all sorts, ranging from target practice to singing, dancing, listening to music, and of course dining. When Henry VIII died in 1547, his funeral train stretched for four miles, reaching from London to Windsor's St. George's Chapel, where he was entombed.[8]

Henry VIII's daughter, Queen Elizabeth I, spent much of her reign at Windsor. She liked the safety of the castle. It provided protection from the many enemies who wanted her throne, and from the dreaded "black death," the plague that was unfurling like a heavy blanket across London. While she lived there, Elizabeth I held lavish parties to entertain foreign dignitaries and the knights of the Garter. She enjoyed music, dancing, and theatrical entertainment. The story goes that she even commissioned William Shakespeare to write *The Merry Wives of Windsor* so that it could be performed during one of her Garter feasts at the castle.[9] While Elizabeth was in power, she commissioned several building projects at Windsor, including the North Terrace and the Gallery that overlooked it.

More than any other monarch before him, Charles I was a connoisseur of fine art. He adorned Windsor Castle with paintings, sculptures, fountains, and fine furniture. A clock was even installed in the clock tower during his reign. Though Charles might have been considered a good decorator, he wasn't considered a good king. His arguments with Parliament eventually led to civil war. Charles was taken captive and held prisoner at Windsor Castle; and then, on January 30, 1649, he was beheaded outside of Whitehall in London.

Following his death, the monarchy was dissolved for a time. A man named Oliver Cromwell named himself Lord Protector of the government. He sold many of the fine works of art at Windsor to help pay the country's debt. He even tried to sell the castle itself, but Parliament halted the sale by a narrow margin of just a few votes. After Cromwell's death in 1658, his son assumed the role of Lord Protector. By 1660, it was clear that the people found this form of government no better than one run by a king, so the monarchy was restored. Charles I's son, Charles II, became the new king.[10]

BECOMING A KNIGHT

Arms of the Order of the Garter

Generally, a knight was a son of a noble family. From birth, the young man would receive specific training from his parents. He would be expected to have good manners and display qualities of bravery and loyalty. A future knight would become a page by age seven. In this role, he would serve the lord and lady of the castle. He would also be educated in the royal demands of knighthood. He would be taught how to ride a horse, and how to fight while doing so. Training typically began on the back of a wooden horse.

By the time the future knight reached the age of 14, he would be heralded as a squire. In this position, he would serve a knight and would learn all the skills of knighthood: how to use weapons and how to wear armor; and how to act properly at social functions, including learning etiquette at state dinners, how to dance, and how to treat ladies appropriately.

At age 21, a successful squire would become a knight. From that point on, he would be expected to lead battles, act chivalrous in all his interactions with others, and train future knights. If he was particularly impressive in his knighthood, he would be invited to become one of the 26 members of the Order of the Garter.

CHAPTER 3

creating a fantasy castle

During the reign of Charles II, Windsor Castle was transformed into a luxurious palace in the latest European Baroque style. To do the work, the king hired architect Hugh May, artist Antonio Verrio, and woodcarver Grinling Gibbons, the master carver to the Crown. First, the interior of the State Apartments was changed to show that the king wanted to be more accessible to his court. Charles I had been seen as cold and distant, so Charles II tried to appear more approachable. The rooms were laid out in a specific sequence, beginning with large, more public rooms and then moving into smaller and smaller rooms until visitors reached the private room of the

Exterior of the State Apartments

The King's Drawing Room at Windsor Castle has been the monarch's private abode to entertain special guests since Charles II's reign.

king. Only the most important court officials could get as far as the king's personal quarters.

In addition to the architectural changes, the State Apartments were also elaborately decorated. Verrio painted exquisite murals and ceilings in the King's Dining Room, the Queen's Presence Chamber, and the Queen's Audience Chamber. Gibbons carved fine woods into three-dimensional images of animals, plump fruit and vegetables, delicate flowers, and angelic cherubs. These features are still part of the beauty of Windsor Castle.[1]

The 1700s were a rather low time for Windsor Castle. The monarchs who reigned during this era did not use the castle very often. In fact, it became so rundown that people who lived and worked in the town used parts of the grounds as a thoroughfare. Artwork from the time period shows the castle gates wide open (one gate is even removed), traveling merchants running businesses near the grounds, and peasants moving back and forth between the castle and the surrounding area.[2]

In 1778, King George III and his family moved back to Windsor and began work on its restoration. At this time, England was in the middle of a great war on the other side of the Atlantic. Just a few years before, the American Founding Fathers had sent King George III the Declaration of Independence, outlining his unfair treatment of the colonies. By 1778, the Revolutionary War was in full swing.

While he was unpopular abroad, King George III wasn't necessarily unpopular in England. Known as one of the most cultured of all the monarchs, he started the Royal Academy of Arts, became the first monarch to study science as part of his education, and became interested in agriculture, earning himself the nickname "Farmer George."[3] He also purchased a house in London for his wife, which eventually became known as the beloved royal residence Buckingham Palace.

Buckingham Palace

During the renovations at Windsor Castle, the royal family lived on the castle grounds in the Queen's Lodge (which was demolished in 1823). This suited George III just fine, considering he loved the countryside and the lodge allowed his family to be closer to it. George III had a mental illness that eventually made him unsuitable to be king. By the time he passed away at Windsor Castle on January 29, 1820, he was suffering greatly from his illness and was also completely blind and deaf. The monarch who had reigned for nearly 60 years (the third longest in British history) had a very sad end indeed.[4]

In 1824, George IV (George III's son) was the reigning monarch in England. His renovations at Windsor Castle created a legacy that continues to be enjoyed. He wanted to create almost a "fantasy" castle, one that would have been found in illustrated fairytales. Up to that time, the exterior of Windsor was a mishmash of styles—the result of many renovations over hundreds of years. George IV sought to give the castle a more universal, Gothic style. He added turrets and battlements. He decorated plain stone walls with parapets and arrow loops. He added gargoyles to the roofline and Gothic arches over the windows. The famous Round Tower wasn't majestic enough for his tastes, so he added another thirty feet to its height.

While he remade the outside with a medieval flair, he redesigned the inside to be modern, comfortable, and luxurious. During his reign, the French Revolution was going on across the English Channel. George was able to capitalize on the unrest, purchasing some of the French monarchy's finest treasures for Windsor Castle. One of George IV's greatest legacies is his Waterloo Chamber, which celebrated the British victory over Napoleon at the Battle of Waterloo in 1815. While King George IV was not actually present at the battle, the artwork found in this room gives the impression that he was. This famous room is still used for important state functions.[5]

In 1837, the young Victoria came to Windsor for the first time as Queen of England. A few years later, she married Prince Albert, and the couple spent their honeymoon at Windsor Castle. They continued to spend many months of the year there with their young family. The queen wasn't altogether fond of London and preferred spending her time in the countryside. Prince

Queen Victoria and her husband Prince Albert were devoted parents who enjoyed spending many months of the year with their family at Windsor Castle.

Albert enjoyed the outdoors, too. He set up a small farm on the castle grounds for breeding different livestock and conducting various experiments with agricultural crops.

The family entertained often in the castle. The queen was related in some way to just about every royal family in Europe, so these gatherings were almost like family reunions. One guest was Tsar Nicholas I, who visited in June 1844. Another was Louis Philipe of France, who came the following

Queen Victoria and Princess Beatrice in the Queen's Sitting Room in 1895

year. The British monarchy mainly held balls, concerts, and banquets at Windsor.

In 1848, the family showcased a Shakespearean performance of *The Merchant of Venice* in the castle's Rubens Room. It was such a memorable experience that the royal family made it a tradition. From that point through 1860, a play was performed at Windsor Castle every Christmas. Then, just before Christmas in 1861, Prince Albert died at Windsor Castle. The queen was devastated by this sudden loss and spent the rest of her life in mourning. She was shrouded in black for the next 40 years, earning her the moniker the "Widow of Windsor." Queen Victoria died in January 1901, and her state funeral was held at Windsor.[6]

A CASTLE UNDER SIEGE

Medieval catapult

Windsor Castle came under siege only three times in its history: in 1193, 1216, and 1263. When armies attacked a castle, they usually bombarded the walls with huge boulders fired from giant catapults. The enemy soldiers shot arrows at the people on the castle's roof. They also tried to climb the walls using ladders and machines that looked like towers on wheels. Battering rams were also used to try to break through doors or stone walls.

Inside the castle, drawbridges were raised so that no one could cross the motes—ditches filled with rancid water and vermin. The heavy wooden grille of the Barbican entrance would also have been closed tight. "Murder holes" would be manned as well. Through these small openings at the tops of the gates, large rocks, hot sand, and burning oil could be dumped on any would-be intruders. The defending soldiers would shoot their arrows through the "arrow loop" windows. These small slits allowed arrows to get out while protecting the shooter inside.

A castle siege could last days, weeks, or even months. During the siege, the people inside the castle couldn't leave or receive food and supplies. They had to have enough of everything within the castle walls to support them for the length of the siege. When one side ran out of equipment, men, or supplies, the fight was over. If the people in the castle gave up, then the castle and its inhabitants would be captured by the invading army.

CHAPTER 4

the house of windsor

Ever since George I had ruled England, the British royal family had claimed some kind of German ancestry. Even Prince Albert, Victoria's beloved husband, was from Germany. When World War I broke out in 1917, Great Britain and its allies were fighting Germany and its allies. King George V had to show that the British family was English without any German sympathies.

On July 17, 1917, King George V officially gave himself and his offspring the surname Windsor. From that point on, his descendants would be part of the House of Windsor. This was a revolutionary idea. Before this declaration, a royal "house" or "dynasty" had never been named after a building. They were usually

This political cartoon from 1917 shows King George sweeping away his German titles. "Good riddance" he seems to be saying. This was the beginning of the "House of Windsor."

named after a geographic area, such as Normandy or York. Windsor Castle had made history once again.[1]

When King George VI became king in 1936, he and his wife, Queen Elizabeth (later known as the Queen Mother), and their children already lived in the Royal Lodge in the Windsor Great Park area. They considered Windsor their home, and it never felt out of place for them to stay at Windsor Castle. However, during World War II, the king and queen decided to live at Buckingham Palace in London. The rest of their capital city's citizens were being tormented nightly by Germany's incessant bombing. Called blitzkrieg, or "lightning war," the Germans had already successfully used this military strategy against several countries, including Poland, Denmark, France, Yugoslavia, and Greece. Now they were trying to get the British to surrender.

Instead of taking refuge behind the stone fortress of Windsor Castle, King George and Queen Elizabeth stayed in London with their people. The

Firefighters struggle against a fire in London after another bombing during "The Blitz" in 1941.

palace was bombed nine times during the war, but still the king and queen stayed, showing Germany and the rest of the world that the German bombs would have no impact on their daily lives. However, the royal daughters, Princess Elizabeth and Princess Margaret, were kept for safety at Windsor Castle and spent most of their childhood there. During this time, many other children in London were also rushed out of the city for safety. They stayed with extended family across the Atlantic in Canada or in the English countryside, far from the bombings.[2]

Princess Elizabeth became Queen Elizabeth II in 1953. And in an odd way, World War II can be credited for her deep affection for Windsor Castle. After all, it was the place where she formed her earliest memories. Some of these memories are the pantomimes that she and Princess Margaret performed for their parents every Christmas from 1941 to 1944. In Great Britain, pantomimes are plays for child actors that are generally based on fairy tales and include music, jokes, and comedy. They are usually performed around Christmas. The royal sisters would enlist the help of their schoolmates at the Royal School of Windsor. They would all dress up in grand costumes and perform special shows like *Cinderella, Sleeping Beauty,* and *Aladdin* for their parents and other guests in the famous Waterloo Chamber. These weren't just thrown-together productions. They were written and directed by their school's headmaster, or principal, and included printed programs. The last play, *Old Mother Red Riding Boots,* performed in 1944, was actually written by the princesses and one of their friends.[3] Photographs of the play that were auctioned in 2013 raised 3,200 pounds, or about $5,300.[4]

On February 6, 1952, King George VI died in his sleep. He was only 56 years old. People around the world were deeply saddened by the news. Memorial services were even held in churches in the United States, and the Stars and Stripes there were flown at half-mast in the king's honor. Throughout World War II, people had admired the king for his honor, bravery, and patriotism. A television documentary from the time period said, "It could be said of him [King George VI] that as long as he lived, he was the guiding star of a brave nation, and when he died, the little children cried in the streets."[5]

Three queens, Queen Elizabeth II (left), Queen Mary, and Queen Elizabeth, the Queen Mother, mourn the loss of King George VI at his funeral.

As he lay in state at Westminster Hall, hundreds of thousands of Brits stood outside in the cold winter weather waiting in mile-long lines just to pay respects to their king. On the day of the funeral, the procession wound from Westminster through the streets of London to Paddington Station; from there the coffin was transported by train to Windsor Castle. The lawns, steps, and courtyards at Windsor were covered in thousands of wreaths and flower bouquets sent from people all over the world as a tribute to the king.[6] George VI was buried at St. George's Chapel, just like many of the British monarchs who had served before him. Fifty years later, in 2002, his wife, Queen Elizabeth (the Queen Mother) would be laid to rest by his side.

QUEEN MARY'S DOLLS' HOUSE

The dollhouse ready to ship

Queen Mary was the wife of King George V and mother to King George VI. In the 1920s, a special gift was commissioned for her: a five-foot-tall dollhouse. Her cousin, Princess Marie Louise, came up with the idea for the gift because she thought it would be a nice way for the people of Great Britain to thank their queen for her sacrifices during World War I. A dollhouse with small furniture, small dishes, and small accessories would be the perfect gift for Queen Mary, since she was known to love tiny treasures.

The architect of the dollhouse was Sir Edwin Luytons. It was a 1-to-12-scale model of a real aristocratic house from the 1920s. It included a yard, which was revealed by opening a drawer at the bottom of the house. It also had a wine cellar (with tiny bottles of real wine). It had working electricity with brass light switches, and plumbing with running water in the sinks and a flushing toilet. Approximately 1,500 artists contributed items to the house, including Cartier, who designed a longcase clock for one of the home's marble hallways.

Famous authors of the day also contributed some of their works to the house's library. These miniature books were printed in the best quality and organized according to traditional library standards on the room's ornate shelves. The dollhouse even had mini vinyl records and a record player in the music room, a real working lawn mower in the garden, miniature Rolls-Royce cars in the garage, and crown jewels, with real diamonds and rubies, locked in a vault.

Queen Mary's Dolls' House remains at Windsor Castle and is one of the most popular exhibits, especially among the castle's young visitors.

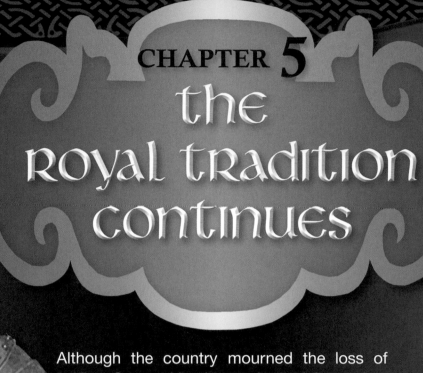

CHAPTER 5
the
royal tradition
continues

Although the country mourned the loss of King George VI, citizens looked forward to the coronation of the next monarch. In an official ceremony at Westminster Abbey on June 2, 1953, Princess Elizabeth was crowned queen. A formal proclamation was read that day outside the abbey gates: "God Save the Queen."[1]

As the reigning monarch of Great Britain, Queen Elizabeth II has many official residences, and Windsor Castle is one of them. She uses the castle as both a home where her family can spend time together and as a place where she can perform certain royal duties. Throughout the year, she generally spends her weekends at Windsor Castle. She also spends a month there, March through April,

The Long Walk leading to Windsor Castle

Knights are sworn into the Order of the Garter in the ornate Garter Room at Windsor.

for an event known as Easter Court. During this time, the queen hosts special events for guests called "dine and sleeps." These include lavish dinners, banquets, and balls that last so late into the evening that the guests are invited to spend the night in the elegant guest rooms. Later, during the month of June, the Queen returns to Windsor for a week. This is when she attends the annual Order of the Garter service at St. George's Chapel. Before the service, she hosts a luncheon for the knights inside the Waterloo Chamber.

Also in June, she stays at Windsor for the Royal Ascot Racecourse, a traditional horse race that Queen Anne began in 1711. The events span five days. Each day opens with the Queen and the royal family arriving in horse-drawn carriages.

When important guests come to town, such as foreign heads of state, the Queen often hosts them at Windsor Castle. They are treated in grand style. They are driven into the castle yard in a horse-drawn carriage, where they are met by a military honor guard. Some of the guests who have been given this special treatment include President and Mrs. Mbeki of South Africa in 2001, President and Madame Chirac of France in 2004, and King Abdullah II and Queen Rania of Jordan in 2001.[2]

In March 2014, the Queen's grandson, Prince William of Wales, hosted a star-studded charity event at Windsor Castle. Emma Watson, Cate Blanchett, Benedict Cumberbatch, and dozens of other celebrities all gathered to support the Royal Marsden Hospital, the first hospital in the world dedicated to cancer treatment and research. The gala also honored Ralph Lauren, the American designer, whose generous donation to the hospital helped fund a

Prince William with actress Emma Watson (center) and model Kate Moss (right). Sometimes celebrities are invited to events at Windsor Castle.

new breast cancer research center. This event was the first of its kind to be held at Windsor Castle.[3]

To prepare for all these events, the Great Kitchen becomes a whirlwind of activity. This is the oldest working kitchen in all of England. It has served food to 32 of the 40 monarchs who have lived in the castle over the last 750 years. The copper pots are 200 years old, and the large kitchen whisk can scramble up to 250 eggs at a time. The kitchen staff is extensive, as would be expected with the number of royal family members, guests, and staff who need to be fed when the Queen is in residence. There are 33 regular staff members, 20 chefs and sous chefs, three pastry chefs, and 10 porters. The staff sometimes spends six months planning and preparing meals for state banquets, which often serve 160 guests at a time. Just to make sure everything in the kitchen—and the castle—runs like "clockwork," the clocks in the kitchen are set five minutes fast. That guarantees that the queen is never waiting for her food.[4]

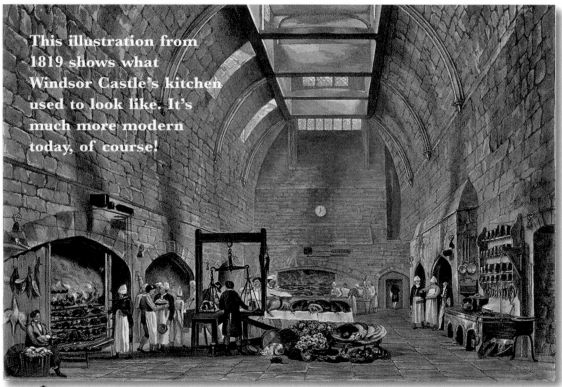

This illustration from 1819 shows what Windsor Castle's kitchen used to look like. It's much more modern today, of course!

Windsor Castle is the largest continuously occupied castle in the world. It has a rich history that stretches back nearly 1,000 years. That is why it was so devastating when the fire erupted in 1992. Yet, this wasn't the end for Windsor Castle.

Once the fire was extinguished and the damage was assessed, plans for reconstruction began. When it was all finished, it was believed to be the largest restoration project to be undertaken anywhere during the 20th century. Despite its magnitude, the project was completed in less than five years. A celebration of its completion coincided with Queen Elizabeth's and Prince Philip's 50th Golden Wedding Anniversary.

Queen Elizabeth II and her husband Prince Philip

Just before the royal celebration, the Queen held a private party for the 1,500 workers who had been employed on the project. She told them how delighted she was with their masterful craftsmanship. At the formal anniversary party, a lavish ball was held in one of the rooms that had received the most damage—St. George's Hall. The restoration was a perfect success. In fact, the Queen's son, Prince Charles, later told the press that the restorations on that particular room were "absolutely breathtaking."[5] In St. George's Hall, a false ceiling had been added, which hid the beautiful fanned timberwork of the original ceiling. When the room was restored, the

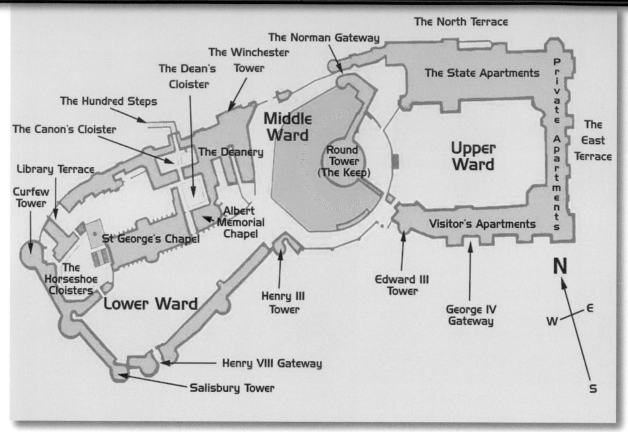

The North Terrace

The Norman Gateway

The Winchester

The Dean's   Tower

Cloister

The Hundred Steps

The Canon's Cloister

The State Apartments

Middle
Ward

The Deanery

Round
Tower
(The Keep)

Upper
Ward

Private Apartments

The
East
Terrace

Library Terrace

Curfew
Tower

Albert
Memorial
Chapel

St George's Chapel

Visitor's Apartments

The
Horseshoe
Cloisters

Lower Ward

Henry III
Tower

Edward III
Tower

N

George IV
Gateway

W

E

Henry VIII Gateway

Salisbury Tower

S

Visitors to Windsor Castle refer to tourist maps like this one to help them see the sights.

ceiling was re-created in its original Gothic style. Several other interesting features of the castle were uncovered during the restoration: a well that extended down toward the Thames, and an undercroft in St. George's Hall that had been used to store wine and provisions in the 1300s.[6]

Windsor Castle will always hold a special place in the hearts of the royal family and the people of Great Britain. Its imposing physical presence, with its grand stone structures and ornate interiors, stands as a reminder of the rich history of the people and the great monarchs who have ruled them. Windsor Castle is truly a British national treasure.

THE NEXT
IN LINE

Prince George

Life at Windsor Castle continues today just as it did during previous monarchical reigns. Queen Elizabeth still resides there, and she is often joined by visits from her children, grandchildren, and great grandchildren. Windsor Castle is filled with the heritage of the past and continues to be a place where memories are created.

The next in line for the British throne is Prince Charles, the Prince of Wales. He is followed by his eldest son, Prince William of Wales. Third in line for succession is one of the newest members of the royal family, Prince George of Cambridge. Born in July 2013, he is the first child of Prince William of Wales and Kate Middleton, who are also known as the Duke and Duchess of Cambridge.

Prince George has spent many happy days so far during his visits at Windsor Castle. In fact, in the summer of 2014, he hosted some playdates there. These kid parties have included visits from his cousins and his godmother's children.

Windsor Castle, with its high stone walls and secluded acreage, is the perfect place for the young royal to enjoy some peace and quiet. His parents prefer not having the paparazzi photograph his life, and Windsor Castle gives them the privacy they desire. Prince George is free to play and enjoy life at Windsor Castle just as his royal family has done for centuries before him.

1070	William the Conqueror chooses a site for a new castle. On the edge of his royal hunting grounds, it is the highest point for miles around, which gives it a strategic advantage.
1170s	Henry II rebuilds parts of the castle, replacing the earlier wood construction with stone.
1312	Edward III is born at Windsor Castle.
1348	Edward III starts the Order of the Garter at Windsor. This organization is meant to reward those who have shown loyalty to the Crown and have displayed military merit.
1360s	Edward III has St. George's Hall built for use by the Garter Knights.
1475	Edward IV begins construction on St. George's Chapel. It is completed by Henry VIII.
1483	Edward IV dies and is buried at St. George's Chapel.
1500s	English monarchies begin to prefer other residences to castle life.
1642	Oliver Cromwell takes over Windsor Castle after the Battle of Edgehill. He tries to start a republic and begins to sell the castle's artwork and precious possessions. Windsor Castle itself is nearly sold.
1648	Charles I is captured and held captive at Windsor Castle; he is beheaded in London and then returned to St. George's Chapel for burial.
1670s	Charles II constructs the new State Apartments, including the King's Dining Room, the Queen's Presence Chamber, and the Queen's Audience Chamber.
1770s	Windsor falls into a state of disrepair. Parts of the grounds practically become a public thoroughfare.
1778	George III and his royal family move to Windsor into the Queen's Lodge while the castle is being restored.
1823	The Queen's Lodge is demolished.
1824	George IV's renovations on the castle begin. One of the most impressive additions is the Waterloo Chamber.
1840s	Queen Victoria's young family lives at Windsor.
1845	Queen Victoria decides to open the State Apartments to the public.
1861	Prince Albert dies at Windsor Castle. The mourning Queen Victoria becomes known as the Widow of Windsor.
1917	At the beginning of World War I, the royal family's German surname is abandoned and the new name, House of Windsor, is chosen.
1924	Queen Mary's Dolls' House is finished as a gift for Queen Mary, the wife of King George V.
1940s	Princesses Elizabeth and Margaret Rose dwell in the safety of Windsor Castle during World War II.
1952	King George VI is buried in St. George's Chapel.
1992	A great fire sweeps through Windsor, severely damaging or destroying one-fifth of the castle.
1997	The restoration of Windsor Castle is complete at a cost of 37 million pounds ($59.2 million).
2002	The Queen Mother, Queen Elizabeth, is buried in St. George's Chapel.
2003	Prince William of Wales celebrates his 21st birthday at Windsor Castle.
2005	Prince Charles and Camilla Parker-Bowles are married in a religious ceremony at St. George's Chapel.
2013	Prince George of Cambridge is born, becoming third in line to the throne.
2014	Queen Elizabeth and the royal family continue to spend many of their weekends at Windsor Castle.

Introduction. Fire!

1. "Windsor Castle Fire—November 20, 1992," *Fire Service* UK, http://www.fireservice.co.uk/history/windsor-castle-fire

2. "The Great Fire at Windsor," *The London Studios,* November 22, 1992, http://www.youtube.com/watch?v=D-Od9doJbWY

3. Ibid.

Chapter 1. A Fortress on a Hill

1. "William the Conqueror," *BBC History,* http://www.bbc.co.uk/history/historic_figures/william_i_king.shtml

2. "Windsor Castle," *Royal Collection Trust,* http://www.royalcollection.org.uk/sites/default/files/Windsor_Castle_Fact_Sheet.pdf

3. "The Castle," *British History Online,* http://www.british-history.ac.uk/report.aspx?compid=43178

4. "Windsor Castle," *Royal Collection Trust,* http://www.royalcollection.org.uk/sites/default/files/Windsor_Castle_Fact_Sheet.pdf

5. David Nash Ford, "Windsor, Royal Town & Castle," *Britannia,* http://www.britannia.com/history/berks/windsor.html

6. "Who Built the Castle?" *Royal Collection Trust,* http://www.royalcollection.org.uk/visit/windsorcastle/about/who-built-the-castle

7. "John (c.1167–1216)," *BBC History,* http://www.bbc.co.uk/history/historic_figures/john.shtml

Chapter 2. The Merry Years at Windsor

1. "The Castle," *British History Online,* http://www.british-history.ac.uk/report.aspx?compid=43178

2. "A Short History of St. George's," *College of St. George at Windsor Castle,* http://www.stgeorges-windsor.org/about-st-georges/history.html

3. "Windsor Castle," *The Official Website of the British Monarchy,* https://www.royal.gov.uk/TheRoyalResidences/WindsorCastle/WindsorCastle.aspx

4. "St. George," *Britannia History,* http://www.britannia.com/history/stgeorge.html

5. "St. George's Chapel," *Royal Borough of Windsor & Maidenhead,* http://www.windsor.gov.uk/things-to-do/st-georges-chapel-p45153

6. "Windsor Castle—World's Oldest and Largest Inhabited Castle," BBC The Queen's Palaces, http://www.youtube.com/watch?v=WRNIoXtWEew

7. "Royal Burials in the Chapel by Location," College of St. George, http://www.stgeorges-windsor.org/about-st-georges/royal-connection/burial/burials-in-the-chapel-by-location.html

8. "The Castle," British History Online.

9. Ibid.

10. "Windsor Castle—World's Oldest and Largest Inhabited Castle."

Chapter 3. Creating a Fantasy Castle

1. "Windsor Castle—World's Oldest and Largest Inhabited Castle," *BBC The Queen's Palaces,* http://www.youtube.com/watch?v=WRNIoXtWEew

2. Ibid.

3. "George III," *The Official Website of the British Monarchy,* http://www.royal.gov.uk/historyofthemonarchy/kingsandqueensoftheunitedkingdom/thehanoverians/georgeiii.aspx

4. "Windsor Castle—World's Oldest and Largest Inhabited Castle."

5. Ibid.

6. "The Castle," *British History Online,* http://www.british-history.ac.uk/report.aspx?compid=43178

Chapter 4. The House of Windsor

1. "The Royal Family Name," *The Official Website of the British Monarchy,* https://www.royal.gov.uk/thecurrentroyalfamily/theroyalfamilyname/overview.aspx

2. "Windsor Castle," *Royal Collection Trust,* http://www.royalcollection.org.uk/sites/default/files/Windsor_Castle_Fact_Sheet.pdf

3. Maev Kennedy, "Young Elizabeth and Margaret: Pantomime Dames," *The Guardian,* December 3, 2013, http://www.theguardian.com/uk-news/2013/dec/03/queen-elizabeth-margaret-pantomime-photos

4. "Queen and Princess Margaret Panto Photos Sell for 3,200 Pounds," *BBC News England,* December 11, 2013, http://www.bbc.co.uk/news/uk-england-25333177

5. "Accession and Coronation," *The Official Website of the British Monarchy,* http://www.royal.gov.uk/HMTheQueen/AccessionCoronation/Accessionandcoronation.aspx

6. Ibid.

Chapter 5. The Royal Tradition Continues

1. "Accession and Coronation," *The Official Website of the British Monarchy,* http://www.royal.gov.uk/HMTheQueen/AccessionCoronation/Accessionandcoronation.aspx

2. "Windsor Castle," *The Official Website of the British Monarchy,* https://www.royal.gov.uk/TheRoyalResidences/WindsorCastle/WindsorCastle.aspx

3. "Prince William Hosts Huge Charity Event at Windsor Castle," *The Telegraph,* n.d., http://www.telegraph.co.uk/news/uknews/prince-william/10829024/Prince-William-hosts-huge-charity-event-at-Windsor-Castle.html

4. Royal Collection Trust: "Tour the Great Kitchen," http://www.royalcollection.org.uk/event/tour-to-the-great-kitchen

5. Ray Moseley, "On Fire's Fifth Anniversary, Windsor Castle Sparkles," *Chicago Tribune,* November 18, 1997, http://articles.chicagotribune.com/1997-11-18/news/9711180043_1_windsor-castle-queen-and-philip-restoration

6. Ibid.

Books

100 Treasures of Windsor Castle. London: Royal Collections Publications, 2010.

Boyer, Crispin. *National Geographic Kids Everything Castles: Capture These Facts, Photos, and Fun to Be King of the Castle!* Washington, DC: National Geographic Children's Books, 2011.

Mortimer, Ian. *The Time Traveler's Guide to Medieval England: A Handbook for Visitors to the Fourteenth Century.* New York: Simon & Schuster, 2009.

Queen Mary's Dolls' House: Official Guidebook. London: Royal Collections Publications, 2010.

Windsor Castle Official Souvenir Guide. London: Royal Collections Publications, 2010.

Works Consulted

British History Online, http://www.british-history.ac.uk/report.aspx?compid=43178

The British Royals, http://www.britroyals.com

College of St. George at Windsor Castle, http://www.stgeorges-windsor.org/about-st-georges/history.html

Ford, David Nash. "Windsor, Royal Town & Castle," *Britannia,* accessed February 9, 2014, http://www.britannia.com/history/berks/windsor.html

"Founding Knights of the Order of the Garter," *Oxford Dictionary of National Biography,* accessed February 9, 2014, http://www.oxforddnb.com/templates/theme-print.jsp?articleid=92770

"The Great Fire at Windsor," *The London Studios* 22/11/92, You-Tube video, accessed February 9, 2014, http://www.youtube.com/watch?v=D-Od9doJbWY

"John (c.1167–1216)," *BBC History,* accessed February 9, 2014, http://www.bbc.co.uk/history/historic_figures/john.shtml

Kennedy, Maev. "Young Elizabeth and Margaret: Pantomime Dames," *The Guardian,* December 3, 2013, http://www.theguardian.com/uk-news/2013/dec/03/queen-elizabeth-margaret-pantomime-photos

Moseley, Ray. "On Fire's 5th Anniversary, Windsor Castle Sparkles," *Chicago Tribune,* November 18, 1997, http://articles.chicagotribune.com/1997-11-18/news/9711180043_1_windsor-castle-queen-and-philip-restoration

The Official Website of the British Monarchy, http://www.royal.gov.uk/

"Prince William Hosts Huge Charity Event at Windsor Castle." *The Telegraph,* n.d. http://www.telegraph.co.uk/news/uknews/prince-william/10829024/Prince-William-hosts-huge-charity-event-at-Windsor-Castle.html

"Queen and Princess Margaret Panto Photos Sell for 3,200 Pounds," *BBC News England,* December 11, 2013, http://www.bbc.co.uk/news/uk-england-25333177

"Royal Collection Trust, http://www.royalcollection.org.uk/

"St. George," *Britannia History,* accessed February 10, 2014, http://www.britannia.com/history/stgeorge.html

"St. George's Chapel," *Royal Borough of Windsor & Maidenhead,* accessed February 10, 2014, http://www.windsor.gov.uk/things-to-do/st-georges-chapel-p45153

"Windsor Castle: Timeline of Important Events," accessed July 25, 2014, http://www.ancientfortresses.org/windsor-castle-timeline-important-dates.htm

"Windsor Castle—World's Oldest and Largest Inhabited Castle," *BBC The Queen's Palaces,* accessed February 10, 2014,http://www.youtube.com/watch?v=WRNloXtWEew

"Windsor Castle Fire—November 20, 1992," *Fire Service UK,* accessed February 9, 2014, http://www.fireservice.co.uk/history/windsor-castle-fire

On the Internet

BBC: History for Kids
    http://www.bbc.co.uk/history/forkids/

The Official Website of the British Monarchy
    http://www.royal.gov.uk/

Royal Berkshire History for Kids: Windsor Castle
    http://www.berkshirehistory.com/kids/windsor_castle.html

Royal Collection UK: Visit Windsor Castle
    http://www.royalcollection.org.uk/visit/windsorcastle

Royal Collection UK: Windsor Castle—Bring on the Battle
    http://www.royalcollection.org.uk/sites/default/files/Learning_bringonthebattle.swf

Time for Kids: England Timeline
    http://www.timeforkids.com/destination/england/history-timeline

bailey (BAY-lee)—A large fenced courtyard that surrounded the motte and was designed to protect the keep.

Barbican (BAR-bih-kan)—Part of the castle gatehouse that jutted out from the main wall, providing extra defense.

Baroque (buh-ROHK)—A style of art and architecture of Europe that featured ornate detail. It was popular from the early 1600s to the late 1700s.

catapult (KAT-uh-pult)—An ancient weapon used for slinging large rocks over high walls.

cherub (CHAIR-ub)—An angel whose main gift is knowledge.

chivalrous (SHIH-vul-rus)—Behaving like a knight; especially, being courteous and gallant.

fan vault—A type of high ceiling construction using a set of concave ribs spreading out from a central point like an open umbrella.

gargoyle (GAR-goyl)—An ugly carved human or animal face or figure that is generally placed at the gutter of a building to act as a rain spout. This figure is common in Gothic architecture.

Gothic (GAH-thik)—A style of art and architecture of Europe popular between the 12th and 16th centuries that featured height and light.

keep—A central tower at the castle where guards could "keep" watch.

mishmash (MISH-mash)—A jumble of styles, colors, or shapes.

motte (MAHT)—A mound on which the castle keep was built.

page—A young knight in training from around the age of 7 until 14 who served a lord and lady as an attendant.

siege (SEEDJ)—To surround a city or building in order to take control of it.

squire—A teenaged knight-in-training who served as an apprentice to a full knight.

undercroft (UN-der-kroft)—An underground room, especially one under a church.

index